D0501768

To _____

From _____

*I'll always be glad*
*we're sisters!*

WE MUST LAUGH & WE MUST SING. WE ARE BLEST BY EVERYTHING. EVERYTHING WE LOOK UPON IS BLEST

# Because You're My Sister

## Illustrated by
## Mary Engelbreit

**Andrews McMeel
Publishing**

Kansas City

is a registered trademark of
Mary Engelbreit Enterprises, Inc.

ISBN: 0-8362-3676-9

Written by Jan Miller Girando

# Because You're
# My Sister

The older we get,
the wiser we are—
the more that we value those few
who have always been there
to support and to care,
and to help with whatever we do.

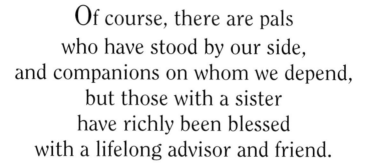

Of course, there are pals
who have stood by our side,
and companions on whom we depend,
but those with a sister
have richly been blessed
with a lifelong advisor and friend.

WE, CANNOT TELL THE PRECISE MOMENT WHEN FRIENDSHIP IS FORMED. AS IN FILLING A VESSEL DROP BY DROP, THERE IS AT LAST A DROP WHICH MAKES IT RUN OVER; SO IN A SERIES OF KINDNESSES THERE IS AT LAST ONE WHICH MAKES THE HEART RUN OVER.

···· JAMES BOSWELL

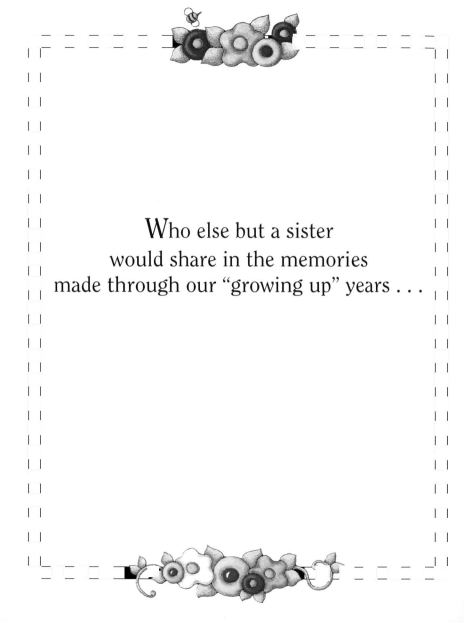

Who else but a sister
would share in the memories
made through our "growing up" years . . .

The Girls

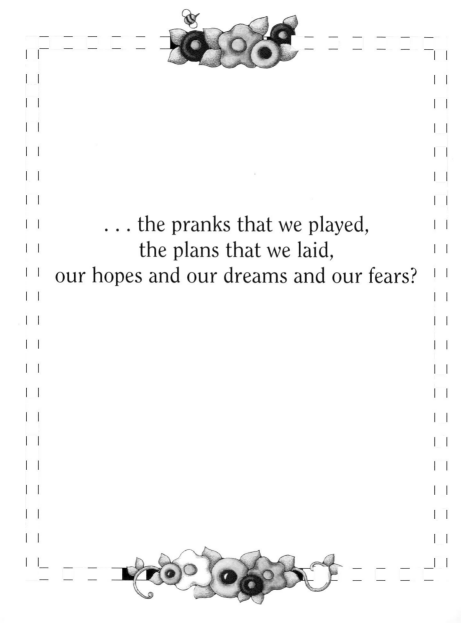

. . . the pranks that we played,
the plans that we laid,
our hopes and our dreams and our fears?

MAKE · A · WISH

Who else but a sister
would know how it feels
when life takes us over the brink?

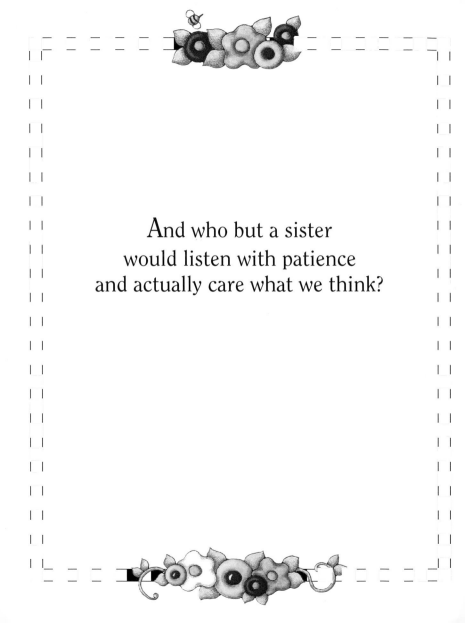

And who but a sister
would listen with patience
and actually care what we think?

GOSSIP

Who else cheers us on
when we're trying our best,
and the perks haven't yet come our way,
and offers encouraging
words of support,
brightening even the cloudiest day?

Who else but a sister
would rush to our side
when misfortune took us by surprise—
helping out, pitching in,
through the thick, through the thin,
doing more than we might realize?

AH! HOW GOOD IT FEELS THE HAND of an OLD FRIEND
· LONGFELLOW ·

And who but a sister
would share in our triumphs
with energy, interest, and zest,
enjoying our victories
as if they were hers,
and pretending to be so impressed?

YOU'RE A

WINNER!

Relaxing is fun when
a sister's around—
lots of good-natured kidding takes place!
We can be who we are,
we can do what we want . . .
or just give one another some space!

·PALS·

When we're trying to weasel
our way out of scrapes,
she just shrugs with a sisterly sigh . . .
and gets set to extend
the warm hand of a friend
should our mischievous plans go awry!

MARNIE AND MAGGIE!

FOR THERE IS NO FRIEND
LIKE A SISTER IN CALM OR
STORMY WEATHER
· CHRISTINA ROSETTI ·

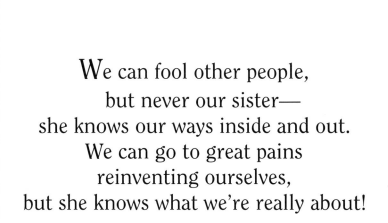

We can fool other people,
but never our sister—
she knows our ways inside and out.
We can go to great pains
reinventing ourselves,
but she knows what we're really about!

That's why sisterly love
is the rarest of gifts,
and its worth is replenished anew
as in laughter and tears
we progress through the years—
I should know, 'cause my sister is you.

WHEN WE ARE GROWN WE'LL SMILE AND SAY
WE HAD NO CARES IN CHILDHOOD'S DAY—
BUT WE'LL BE WRONG. 'TWILL NOT BE TRUE.
I'VE THIS MUCH CARE……I CARE FOR YOU.